KNOCKING FROM INSIDE

KNOCKING
from INSIDE

poems

Tiel Aisha Ansari

The Ecstatic Exchange
2008
Philadelphia

For quotes any longer than those for critical articles and reviews, contact:
The Ecstatic Exchange,
6470 Morris Park Road, Philadelphia, PA 19151-2403
email: abdalhayy@danielmoorepoetry.com

First Edition
ISBN: 978-0-6151-8394-7 (paper)
Published by *The Ecstatic Exchange,*
6470 Morris Park Road, Philadelphia, PA 19151-2403

Acknowledgments:
Journey, Fasting and the *Haiku Ramadan* have appeared in *Islamica Magazine* (Issues #17, 2006 and #20, 2007).
Walk in His Traces won an award in the Islamic Poetry Praise the Prophet competition.
Hearing Voices / Speaking in Tongues won an award from Sol Magazine, Spring 2006 edition.
Others of these poems have previously appeared on Tiel Aisha Ansari's blog: http://knockingfrominside.blogspot.com/

Cover and text design by Abdallateef Whiteman
   www.ianwhiteman.com

Cover photograph © 2003-2007 by Sam Javanrouh
   http://wvs.topleftpixel.com/about.htm

Back cover photograph by Todd Ellner

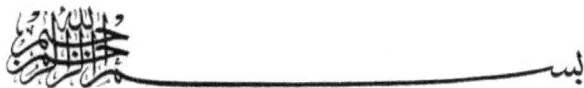

بسم الله الرحمن الرحيم

DEDICATION

For Allah, from Whom all things flow
And for Shaykh Taner Ansari, my connection to Allah
And for Todd, in whom I find Allah every day

CONTENTS

INTRODUCTION

I CAN'T NOW REMEMBER exactly when I became aware of Tiel Aisha Ansari as a presence in the poetry world, and specifically in the Muslim/ Sufi poetry world, but her work has attracted my and others' attention by the suddenness of its authority and relevance. Her artfully "artless" poems with their lyrical moments, more extensive excursions, inner voyages and introspections, momentarily ecstatic realizations and visions, have consistently caught me up in their simplicity of style (though skillfully managing many traditional forms) and limpid straightforwardness of expression. A young poet, in terms of years writing poems (only two by her account), Ansari arrives fully at one with her voice, which loves brevity while digging often quite deep in a relatively short space of poetic time.

Spiritually playful and almost nonchalantly human, each of her poems is a little universe of the speaking heart with the head's reins held taut. And the most arresting thing about her work, for me, is her handling of traditional forms (she loves *sestinas*) without fussiness, and with the same breeziness and clarity in *the natural voice* as her or anyone's use of open form, my usual preference. And it is my usual preference because, except for out-and-out rap and performance poets (who ratchet up rhyme and metric schemes to their highest effective and often astonishing pitch), when poets (or more likely *poetasters*) pour their inspiration into traditional forms they make all kinds of awkward *faux pas*, grammatical transgressions, Victorian word inversions, padding with pronouns or unnecessary adjectives, or force rhyme lines that are there for that reason only, to jangle us with a rhyme ending. It's been argued that poetry in traditional, or "closed" form, is the poetry that people will remember and memorize, to which I must assent. People will probably be reciting "*The Charge of the Light Brigade*" at Kiwanis Club meetings long before they'd be reciting anything by William Carlos Williams. But unless we're writing our poems only for memorization, there's a deeper meaning for the use of both closed form and open form, for the poem as a vehicle for knowledge, contemplation and an opening of the heart-center, a recognition of a new perspective that may have been there all the time, whether within the boundaries of form or not. But Tiel's various schemes, however she approaches the poem at hand, are never forced, but seem to flow organically like the glisten rippling on a summer lake.

One of the formidable challenges for poets with a spiritual bent, and specifically Muslim/Sufi but also Christian and religious Jewish or any other Spiritual Path poets, is a naturalness and heartfeltness, an openness, and particularly a lack of *over-piousness*. Contemporary American Buddhist poets seem to have had the best success in these matters. Most semitically "religious" poetry suffers from a kind of "I know what's coming" piety, an assumption of religiosity that lets the poet get away with poetic murder, in which we are told what we already know, but in verse, with no new nor arresting vision, nor anything even poignantly personal, which amounts in the end to a "religiously correct" sentimentality. In my book, *Cooked Oranges*, I wrote:

> Poetry is what can't be said
> any other way
> Verse is thoughts searching for poetry

In Tiel Ansari's poems we have a definitive line with its definite words, neither more nor less, with no poetic padding, but a kind of bare-bones, no-nonsense ground of being from which the poems emerge – singing. And though generally serene, she doesn't shy away, from time to time, from imaginal wildness.

> Black jackal in the desert giving tongue whose echoes shake the
> hanging cymbals
> in the conqueror's tents: make faint their hearts!
> Vengeful ghosts, come forth across the sand.

But perhaps the most arresting thing about Tiel's work is that she dares to embrace the heart's onflowing imagination, and says "God" without flinching, longs for God or extols God in His creation and in every moment, without hesitation, as naturally as breathing. And she says so with her limpid lyrics in a cultural climate of either agnostic or atheistic doubt in the mainstream poetry world, or misrepresentational hedging in the New Age or pseudo-Sufi world, where the works of a great devotional saint like Rumi are put to emotionally vivid but theologically secular use. When Tiel says "God" she means it, in all her various ways and fresh poetic stratagems, in these poems in which there are many strata, and in this book which contains many gems.

— DANIEL ABDAL-HAYY MOORE

DRINKING FROM THE SOURCE

This verse does not belong to me
my hands are still, my tongue is dumb.
Not composition, memory.

I tried to fashion poetry,
my self-claimed efforts, poorly done.
This verse does not belong to me.

"I have no gift. It's just not me."
"I've tried to write, but it won't come."
Not composition, memory.

The wind blows through the sighing tree,
the surf makes silent rocks a drum.
These voices don't belong to me.

They say it's creativity.
It's not from here. Where is it from?
Not "making up," but memory.

Remembrance is the missing key.
This poetry from elsewhere comes.
These verses don't belong to me
they're written down from memory.

AT HOME IN THE WORLD

A BOX OF WIND

Last night the wind woke me from sleep
rattling the windows, blowing open doors

shaking comfortable certainties.
I went spinning, whirling like a cloud of dust
or was I dancing?

This morning dead leaves swirl in a corner of the building.
They whisper in a language I've forgotten.
What would I know if I could understand the wind?

Bring me a box of wind to carry in my pocket
a murmuring reminder of the language of the sky.
Bring me a box of wind for my bedside table
a music-box to dance to when I dream at night.

And if I should weep,
let my tears be rain in the wind.

TIGER

Mason was the first to go. They said
a tiger found him walking down the trail
behind his house.
                    Then, after he was dead,

Bundy moved into town. His courage failed,
he told me, sitting sweating at the bar.
"The jungle's just... so big. And I feel frail."

He meant to hide among the crowds, the cars,
the man-made smells of sewage, gasoline
from eyes that watched, implacable as stars.

He hoped the city noise, the loud machines
would hide his steps from predatory ears
but tiger senses must have been too keen

to be defeated. Bundy met his fears
just two blocks from a busy liquor store.
No-one saw what happened.
                           All these years,

we never talked about the way it was before:
the tiger cub, the stake and chain, the gin,
the vicious entertainment of the bored

young men we were. We knew it was a sin,
but never guessed at fatal consequence,
avenging angel dressed in tiger-skin.

I'm not a fool, to doubt the evidence
around the corpse, the marks of bloody paws
though older hands say from experience

that my anxiety can have no cause.
"It's twenty years now – tiger cubs forget
and don't come into town." The guilt that gnaws

beneath the fear remains unspoken yet.
They think I lost my nerve. I'll be secure
and happy, once this stinking scow-barge gets

me clear of harbor!
                          What's that, on the shore?
What's moving in the sea, to leave that wake
of moonlight ripples?
                          Let there be no more

delay; the tiger comes aboard to take
what he is owed, and I go willingly
for he is beautiful enough to break
a heart once cracked by its own cruelty.

HEARTBREAKING SPLENDOR

The clouds, like segments of blood-orange scattered
across the dawn sky in its lilac and gold splendor

frame spreading V-tracks of northbound wild geese
who fill the sky with cries of loneliness and splendor

at the ragged end of winter when the storms break up
and the sun emerges to greet the dogwood splendor

of spring, and the blaze of mountain glaciers above
the city skyline, in flawless white-white splendor

draws the eye upwards and upwards and up beyond
the sky and blood-orange clouds to
                              – heartbreaking splendor.

SEAHORSES

There are two kinds of horses in the sea.
One is a little armor-plated fish
that clings to weeds with its curling tail
and looks at you with wise equine eyes.

The other lives only under surf.
Water-colored, clear as glass
you cannot see the great-muscled limbs
that thresh the waves and churn the water to curdled foam.

But in the surf, you may hear the thunder of their hooves.
But in the wind, you may hear their trumpets neighing
and see their manes flying from the broken crests.

And this is no stranger than that fish should be horses!

WINTER WOOD

Here at the dead of winter I turn
to the utter silence of the frozen wood.
Here, in the ice-gripped dripping dark
far from the commerce of silver and gold
there's stillness, finally, if not peace
to soothe or cure a troubled heart.

Here, you can think yourself at the heart
of the world, moveless center of turning.
Here the water is cold and peaceful
and you widen ears that were dull as wood
to hear the far sound of trumpets, golden
announcing the light at the end of the dark –

announcing an end to the trouble and darkness
that weigh so heavy on your weary heart.
Ice can glitter brilliant as gold
and water will shine as bright in its turn
throwing leaf-shadows up into the wood.
Winter and summer, it's all of a piece

and we need these quiet times to appease
the restless demons that stalk in the dark,
that haunt the burning of the summer wood.
Winter is time for the resting heart
to heal, waiting for life to return
waiting for sun and summer's gold.

Dawn breaks with a streak of fugitive gold
and still you worry it. Be at peace.
Search, but leave a few stones unturned
so that the soft things that live in the dark
can flourish a while. Light can be heartless,
betraying the secrets of the winter wood,

revealing truths as bitter as wormwood.
It's true what they say, silence is golden.
Your ears can hear so much less than your heart.
The trees remind you: be still, hold your peace
eat the cold earth, drink water and darkness,
stand still, let your feet feel the earth turning.

A dark sky awaits the sun's return.
Sap stands still in the heart of wood.
The peaceful horizon is limned in gold.

SLEEPERS' TEARS

The Madagascar moth drinks sleepers' tears.
Each insect, merciless, to dreamers brings
the dust of midnight sadness, midnight fears.

They're silent; even waking, you'd not hear
these famished sleep-intruders hovering –
the Madagascar moths that drink your tears –

but in your dreams, you'll feel them circling near,
surrounding you with spectral flutterings
and dust of midnight sadness, midnight fears.

The nightingale's aghast when they appear,
and tries to warn the sleepers. Hear, he sings:
"The Madagascar moth will drink your tears!"

Into your dreams it falls, and falls for years,
the poisoned dust from Madagascan wings –
the dust of midnight sadness, midnight fears.

Tomorrow night perhaps they'll reappear
but now they're gorged on sorrow, staggering.
The Madagascar moth drinks sleepers' tears
and feeds them midnight sadness, midnight fears.

SUMMER STILL LIFE

In gold poppy cups
bumblebees drowse, contented
like sunbathing cats.

KILLDEER

From an empty lot
the cries of startled killdeer
ring like struck glasses.

HEARD OVER THE BACK FENCE

Like a lost letter
a lone note goes wandering
looking for a tune.

BONES OF RIVERS

Ridges of gravel
like bones of ancient rivers
spread out on the sand.

THE FISH'S TALE

I wish I'd never swallowed it – that damned ring
but that's how fish are made. We swallow things.
Something splashes – we just have to look –
it could be food! (It could be just a hook.)
Anyway I rose. Gulp! My fate was sealed,
the scaling-knife, the gutting, the ring revealed.

But I can tell you nothing of the theft,
who stole it from her, why, or why he left
a household full of valuable possessions
and took just the ring. Smacks of obsession,
some high-school sweetheart maybe, spurned, heart-broken
turned stalker, burglar, desperate for this token.

Years later, quite by accident, he finds it.
He'd forgotten – now he's forcibly reminded
of love... teenage angst... a break-and-enter situation.
Oh God, what's the statute of limitations?
He panics, throws the evidence in the drink
safe to forget again – or so he thinks.

Well, he's still safe – no questions will be asked.
She gets her ring back, his misdeed is masked
by my pale entrails. My last gasp brings him relief.
No-one need ever know he was the thief.
And no-one knows my heartfelt dying wish –
that I'd been born as something smarter than a fish.

A DAY AT UNION STATION

Departure
At last, I'm leaving the familiar roof!
I'm undeterred by rain and wind.
This presentation should be quite a feather
in my cap. Eager, I clutch my ticket.
I'm going places. Not letting any grass
grow, not under these clever feet!

Pigeons
We admire one another's tiny coral feet.
Coooooo, coooooo under the roof.
Picking spilled popcorn out of the grass,
we read the news written on the wind...
Freezing tonight? Warmth, that's the ticket.
We'll huddle in the rafters and fluff our feathers.

Arrival
My bags in my hands are light as feathers.
But oh my aching back, my tired feet...
I've grown to hate the sight of a ticket.
Just let me get back under my own roof.
I'm done with blowing about like wind –
time to stay home and mow my own grass.

Porter
Excuse me sir, please don't walk on the grass.
I wish they cared, but they don't give a feather.
I envy travelers, free as the wind.
They go where fancy takes them, rambling feet –
the world to be their home, the sky their roof!
Oh, how I wish I could afford a ticket.

Smoke
You breathe me out, wave me away with your ticket,
I fall from the train stack to blacken the grass.
They scraped years of me from the bright copper roof.
I spread through the air like grey-white feathers.
Clever nets of me coil at your heedless feet –
but oh, I'm helpless prey for a gust of wind.

Agent
Brrr. It's cold at this desk when the wind
blows – Thank you; here's your ticket.
I had a little heater for my feet
but I was careless with the smell of burning grass
you know? Sorry, my head's full of feathers.
Boring job, but it pays for my roof.

Discards
Unused tickets molder in the grass.
Shed feathers scatter before the wind.
Echoes of hurried feet crowd the roof.

THE CITY OF CROWS

rises from the human city
like a tree above its shadow –
combs the air with spreading branches
full of raucous citizens.

Maps laid out in three dimensions,
compass roses round as apples,
chart the windy passages to
where the crows hold parliament.

Riding high on fountain updrafts,
falling then, like stones with feathers,
shooting off along the sidewalk,
settling like black parachutes,

do they watch with raucous laughter
while the roofer climbs his ladder
clinging, terrified of falling,
hapless slave of gravity?

No-one knows the secret business
crows transact on every rooftop.
In their sky-vaulted cathedrals,
do they worship on the wing?

ANCIENT OCEAN

Every desert is haunted by the ghost of an ancient ocean,
phantom surf whispering over the salt remains of a dry ocean.

Invisible waves shatter against the crumbling sandstone reefs
that once reared their heads tall above a storm-tossed ocean.

The lime skeletons of tiny creatures tumble from the air
to be ground to dust by the passing of feet that forget the ocean.

Wind carves waterless ripples into endless expanses of dead sand,
builds dunes on unliving beaches that no longer frame an ocean.

Fossil shells peek from the gravel in dry washes and gullies
like scattered teeth in a shovel of soil from the grave of an ocean.

Over the flats in the distance, the air glitters with heat-mirage
like dazzling reflections from the water of a long-lost ocean.

In the dried mud of the lake-bed, encased in salt and sleeping
the eggs of brine shrimp await the coming of a new ocean.

MOTHER WIND

The wind is a woman with rain in her heart.

The arms of the wind are full of dead leaves.

I am coming, wind. Mother, I am coming

I am racing through the sighing grass.

I am running where the fringe of your shawl sweeps the earth.

The pine wood is howling on the height,

I will meet you at the edge of the cliff.

Will you teach me to fly? Will you teach me to dance?

Mother Wind, I am in your hand.

FISHERMAN DRAGGED TO DEATH BY 150-LB CATFISH: PART I

Now what are we to make of this fish story?
We moralize: "He should have let it go,
not thrown away his life for earthly glory.
It wasn't worth it." Well, that's all you know.
Perhaps a kinder metaphor would show
the fisher struggling, valiant but outweighed
by fateful forces, hidden undertows,
the tragic hero overwhelmed by Fate.
And here's another meaning to relate:
God's service may take all you have to spend.
Hold fast through hardship, hold on to your faith
and do right, though you can't foresee the end.
You're free to choose the meaning as you wish,
pick glory, chance or God to be the fish.

FISHERMAN DRAGGED TO DEATH BY 150-LB CATFISH: PART II

"I'll make you fishers of men," he said.
Never thought it'd come to this –
hooked something I couldn't handle, fell in the water
now I'm being dragged under.
I didn't know what I was signing on for
but I'll hold fast, come what may –
my hook's in God's mouth, and He pulls hard.

A SPECK OF DUST

I saw a ring around the sun this morning,
a million tiny flecks of light, each a miniature sun
embodied in a chip of ice.

Is that what the angels see —
a million human souls, each a tiny fleck of God-fire
embodied in a speck of dust?

ANGEL AT WORK

A homeless man was sitting on a curb,
with half a loaf of bread in shaking hands.
You know the kind – he seemed a bit disturbed –

and passers-by, expecting some demand
of money or compassion, looked away
and walked a little faster. Understand,

that's how we city folk get by each day.
The broken breadcrumbs fell into the street
and pigeons turned, like tigers hearing prey.

They fluttered down and gathered at his feet.
As more and more arrived, with hungry eyes
and razor beaks, all wanting bread to eat –

he looked at them in horrified surprise,
as bolder pigeons started pulling shreds
from slices in his hands. And from the skies

more pigeons came and pecked away his bread –
just half a loaf – worth maybe half a buck –
drew blood from shaking hands and stinking head –

he crumpled helpless, sobbing, shouting "Fuck!
Please help me. Help. Just help. I need, I need –"
– From nowhere, stooping low, a falcon struck.

A feather-storm; a dizzy rush of speed.
The pigeons scattered, angry and afraid
and left a member of their flock to bleed

in cruel claws, beneath the monstrous shade
of wings that brought a falcon here to feed –
of angel wings that came to render aid.

THOSE BLUES

POUR ME WHITE LIGHTNING

In a bar down on Dock Street an old sailor's drinking
He'll drink up his paycheck until it's all gone.
If you'd like to know what the sailor-man's thinking
then sit down beside him and pay for a song.

"Oh, pour me white lightning and chase it with thunder
Pour me salt water with foam on the rocks
Wind and the hailstorm can drag a boat under
May God bring us safe again back to the docks!

"I've followed the salmon through wind and bad weather
I've taken the cod in the teeth of a gale.
I've been an old sailor, come hell or high water
I'll drown in the salt at the end of my tale.

"Man never loved woman with half the devotion
I'll have for the sea when she takes my cold hand.
So bury my bones in the heart of the ocean
For I wasn't made for to sleep on dry land.

"So pour me white lightning and chase it with thunder
Pour me salt water with foam on the rocks
Pray for us sailors and pay the bartender
Drink to my memory down at the docks!"

JOHNNY CASH GOES TO HELL

Well, Johnny he said to St. Peter
"You know that I just can't stay
I'm grateful for all that you've done for me
But I just can't be living this way
while there's people suffering in Hell."

"Well, when I came up here to Heaven
You gave me a suit of white
And I put it on just to please you
But you know that it just ain't right
'cause there's people suffering in Hell."

St. Peter he says to Johnny
"I'm sorry, but those are the rules
I can't let you move out of here, Johnny
Son, what you want me to do
for the people suffering in Hell?"

"Let me play for the damned souls in Hell
Let me play them 'Folsom Prison Blues.'
Let me play for the lost and the struggling
Do the job like I used to do
for the people suffering in Hell."

St. Peter he says to the Devil
"Turn the damned souls out of their cells
The Man in Black, he's a comin'
to give a free concert in Hell
for the people suffering in Hell."

St. Peter he says to Johnny
"I'll send you an angel bodyguard."
Johnny he laughed and said: "Thank you
I ain't scared of no prison yard.
Ain't no-one gonna hurt me in Hell."

The stadium's big as the whole wide Earth
The damned souls were packed ear to ear.
When they heard him say:
Hi!
I'm Johnny Cash!
Well, you should have heard them cheer!
Cheers from the damned souls in Hell!

And a million souls let go their chains
And the souls flew up to the sky.
And when Peter asked: "How do you come here?"
They said: "Johnny Cash made me cry
and I'm done with suffering in Hell."

So Johnny he's wearing the black
And he plays for the damned down in Hell.
And he won't let them send him back to Heaven
Till he empties out every last cell
and there's no-one suffering in Hell
          ...In Hell, in Hell
Johnny's playing the damned out of Hell.

THE REED FLUTE TWELVE-BAR BLUES

They went to the river to cut them some reeds
They went to the river to cut them some reeds
Took a knife to the stalk and they made it bleed.

They put in some holes, the number was nine
They put in some holes, the number was nine
They made it a flute and it sounded so fine.

Ain't but one tune that flute ever played
Ain't but one tune that flute ever played
It cried out to God all through the long day.

Ain't but one word that flute ever said
Ain't but one word that flute ever said
"Take me back, take me back to the old riverbed."

SADNESS WINE

If I invite you to my house, you can expect to dine
and after, you can sit with me and we'll drink sadness wine.

The label's red. The drink is blue. It'll help you kill some time,
the taste's familiar on your tongue, they call it sadness wine.

It could be bitter, could be sweet. But either way, it's fine –
you'll never know the difference once you're drunk on sadness wine.

There's sun and rain and killing frost and black rot on the vine,
and that's what makes the grapes grow rich and full of sadness wine.

The table's spread with soup and bread, but somehow I can't find
a place that's set with more than just a glass of sadness wine.

The phoenix sets itself on fire and leaves the past behind
and someday I will do that too, but now I'm drinking sadness wine.

If you've forgotten what you used to read between the lines,
come sit with me and rest a while, and drink some sadness wine.

TREBLINKA TRAIN BLUES

The train passed by, Lord, a hundred fourteen cars.
The train passed on, good Lord, one hundred fourteen cars.
I saw the silent faces, Lord, all behind the iron bars.

A leaf blew past, Lord, a hand reached out through the grille.
A single leaf blew past, a hand reached for it through the grille.
I saw that hand reach out, Lord, I can see it still.

The leaves were red, my Lord, the train was smoky black.
The leaves were red, good Lord, that evil train was black.
May my God forgive me, I saw that train and turned my back.

GOD TRAIN

God Train rolling in the tunnel
Nowhere run, nowhere hide.
Burning headlamp eye consume you
Take you 'long for the ride.

You hear that distant whistle, make you cry
You don't know why.
It's God Train's voice, make you want to die.

They call you crazy, holy.
God Train make you dance in the street
Sun burn you head and in the dust
Bloody rose grows at you feet.

You hear that distant whistle, make you run
Into the sun.
It's God Train's voice, call you come.

God Train got no track
God Train mind no signal
God Train sell no ticket
Sweet God Train! Call me come.

KNIVES OF SORROW, KNIVES OF JOY

I danced over the knives of sorrow.
I fell on the knives of joy and embraced them.
They cut the same, you know –
one in the other's path.
Ice burns like fire, earth moves like wind.
Never settle for half a glass,
drink bitter with sweet,
dive into a dark well and find it full of stars.

COAST STARLIGHT BLUES

The train rolled in with the sun at her back.
"What news from the south, now what news?"
"I rolled all night, seven hundred miles of track
And all the freight I carried was the blues, lonesome blues
All the freight I carried was the blues."

"Did you bring my love from sunny southern lands?"
"Don't ask me what I did or didn't do.
I rolled all night at the engineer's command
And my wheels were sliding in the dew, frozen dew
My wheels kept sliding in the dew."

A cold, cold wind made the windowpanes rattle.
The station was deserted pretty soon.
That train rolled out headed north to Seattle
And left me with its cargo of the blues, starlight blues
Left me with a freight load of the blues.

LYRIC & BLUES

The Lady from Harlem gave her body and soul
for love of the music, but she couldn't keep control.
They ate out her heart and they wore down her will
'cause the blues, they know how to kill.
But she left us the lyric and blues,
oh, give me that lyric and blues...

Sappho was a slave to art's divine desire
she burned up her life on an incandescent pyre.
She drowned in the ocean that's as dark as the wine
gave it up for a good lyric line.
She had the Illyrican blues.
Oh, give me that lyric and blues...

Big Mama said she would walk on down the road
'cause there ain't no man can bear a woman's load.
Her hound wouldn't hunt and her songs wouldn't pay.
Died poor at the end of the day
with nothing but the lyric and blues.
Oh, give me that lyric and blues...

WHAT ORPHEUS SHOULD HAVE SAID TO EURYDICE

The tide's at ebb, will soon be turning.
We loved full well when it was high.
Now oceanwards your heart is yearning,
don't wait for me when you die.

Beyond the flood Someone draws near
who always loved you more than I.
Then go to greater joy, my dear,
don't wait for me when you die.

A lightless, steep and narrow track
or open skies in which to fly?
Whatever greets you, don't look back.
Don't wait for me when you die.

SORROW TOWN

I've lived long years in Sorrow Town, hear that whistle blow
Every evening when the sun goes down, hear that whistle blow
Got no home in this place called Sorrow, wish I had a ticket on the train
        tomorrow
Lord, Lord, hear that whistle blow.

Rolling over rivers, rolling over plains, hear that whistle blow
Riding through the sunshine, riding through the rain, hear that whistle blow
Day so bright and the night so black, can't find my way to the railroad track
Lord, Lord, hear that whistle blow.

The station's standing empty and the grass grows over the rails
Been too long since this stretch of track has heard that whistle wail
Shadows rise up to drag me down, say "There ain't no train from Sorrow Town
Ain't no train from Sorrow Town!"

Power lines sing with a message for me, hear that whistle blow
God Train coming, gonna set you free, hear that whistle blow
Shake off the dust of Sorrow Land, let the trainman take you by the hand
Lord, Lord, hear that whistle blow!

LISTENING WITH THE HEART

IN PRAISE OF SILENCE

All these words
rushing like wind, flowing like water
burning like fire, bright as the sun
in praise of silence.

Words shake the ground and rattle the heart
tear down mountains, raise tall buildings
echo through green woods
in praise of silence.

In the deep ocean there are no words.
In the heart of the earth there are no words.
In the blackness of space there are no words
but the stars praise silence.

Alone on an empty road at dawn
praise silence.

HEARING VOICES

The poet doesn't invent. He listens.
— JEAN COCTEAU

Listen: what do you hear?
I hear a dead tree weeping in the rain,
sorrow hangs from her naked branches.
In the deep ocean, salmon sing of the return home.
Leaves whisper in the wind's tongue.
I hear cicadas in their strident triumph,
seventeen years of darkness ended at last.
Like a seashell lamenting the distant sea,
I empty myself and echo the world's voices
and call it poetry.

SPEAKING IN TONGUES

This poetry. I never know what I am going to say.
— MEVLANA JELALUDDIN RUMI

I swear I didn't write this —
this vision in a shattered mirror
this symphony for train-whistle, accordion and zither
this feast of knucklebones and armadillo chili,
speech fit only for Harlequin's painted mouth.
Poem? It's more like a blueprint on a crumpled napkin —
for a cathedral designed by Escher and John Cage!
I'm far too sane for that. Someone stole my pen,
scribbled those lines when I wasn't looking,
and signed my name.

INFORMATIONAL DECAY

I heard an echo in a hollow place.
No sound of blowing wind or drifting sand,
some ancient voice was this, a captive trace
of gone-by speech, of argument, demand,
of plea or question, comfort or command.
Long years this message had remained unheard
in empty halls, in untenanted lands,
a letter lost, a homeless, wandering word.
I could not judge it solemn or absurd,
the language, one I'd never learned to speak.
Was it then call of beast or cry of bird
from whiskered mouth, or brightly colored beak?
No. No, this was human speech, now lost.
A warning wasted, at an unknown cost.

HEART MUSIC

Blow gently on my heart; you may hear music
some folk tune, ballad, cheerful melodies.
Blow harder and you might get Harlem jazz
or Sousa marches, brass bands thumping.
(I leave orchestral music to bigger hearts than mine!)
But set it to your ear and hold your breath,
wait for the wind to blow
and you'll hear the blues.

SOUL MUSIC

The lonely desert echoes to a lonely cry,
the same sound reverberates in neon alleyways.
The heart reads its own compass
   and knows no other geography.

Who is it that weeps among the jackals and wolves?

This is the sound of the reed flute wailing.
This is the blues harmonica playing.
This is the tongue of the soul crying out to God.

SEASHELL VOICE

We were a thousand miles from shore,
in some grain-growing state, some prairie town.
I saw a seashell in a dusty store
and picked it up – and could not put it down.
There was no water anywhere around
and yet the surf was rolling in my ear,
a long-forgotten, once-familiar sound.
I thought I smelled the ocean, salt as tears.
Impossible, it seemed the sea drew near,
and waves came whispering along the sand:
"Remember me, oh wandering child, most dear
and keep this echo with you on dry land."
No shell forgets the home that it once knew.
Would that my heart would echo half so true.

MIDNIGHT PRAYER

The fading echoes of a midnight prayer
still faintly audible at break of day
although the supplicant's no longer there

make soft the shadows and make sweet the air.
The morning traffic's noise will drive away
the fading echoes of a midnight prayer

but meantime, linger quiet on the stair
and watch the curtain by the altar sway
although the supplicant's no longer there.

Who knows if it was joy or bleak despair
that brought the sleepless here last night to pray?
The fading echoes of a midnight prayer

leave holiness on wall and rug and chair
a touch of grace, by grace allowed to stay
although the supplicant's no longer there.

You're seeking God? You'll find Him anywhere –
in every house or room whose walls replay
the fading echoes of a midnight prayer
although the supplicant's no longer there.

WILD GEESE

I heard this sound –
              trembling trumpet, heart-breaking, waking, shaking the air
                      with echo ecstatic
              louder than thunder rumbling, rolling, falling golden and fading
to untarnished silver in middle air.
Harbinger, herald of what hallowed approach?
Waiting, bated breath, still-standing heart hearing stillness,
dizzy with dazed anticipation.

In answer rising, dancing from distant horizon, wild wing-wedges widen
overhead the rush and flash of feathered pinions!
Feathered frames encompass compass hearts, trumpet-called to northern shores
              and skies,
guided by pole-stars in their golden eyes.
Follow, hollow hearts, slow feet abandon at trumpet's command –
              guided by pole-stars into far northern skies.

UNDER THE FOREST EAVES

This grove is murmuring in endless, wordless conversation
exchanging news of distant friends and family, I suppose.
Unheard by me, the world-news that every tree here knows
of growth and rise and fall, the fate of vegetative nations.
They silent fall, surround me with some breathless expectation
unmoving now, the flecks of sun on fallen leaves below.
Can vegetable community a human heart enclose
or forest welcome put an end to fleshly isolation?

I held my breath. The trees and I stood still, anticipating
and on my lips and in my heart there silent rang a Name.
And in the stillness of the trees – I thought I heard the same.
No tree can speak in human tongue, nor human understand them,
but Who we humans answer to is also Who commands them.
– And so I learned one day when I with trees stood breathless waiting.

NO WORDS

When you place my stone

let there be no words on it

just an empty cup.

CHANGES

WAKING

Did you not know, when the hill
rolled up out of the fog like a monster ship
or was it an iceberg? ... Anyway,
harbinger of disaster. Did you not know?
Did you not see the rivers streaming down her flanks
as she breached, jaws opening on the world –
cavernous throat lit by strange interior suns –
did you not see rough slouching?
Did you feel time unraveling underfoot,
clocks running backward, words following echoes,
work undone, pictures restored to virgin white?
Did you feel nothing?

Waken into a changed world. Set your clock
by the sun: climb the hill to watch for moonrise.
Learn to live on unsteady ground. See the fog
burning gold in the morning when you wake.

RAIN AND MEMORY

In memory, savannahs roll out dry
and empty underneath a dust-stained sky
where lions hide in lion-colored grass
and evenings echo to the jackal's cry.
But here the rain comes rolling down the glass
and auto wheels hiss wetly as they pass.
I sleep to gurgling music in the gutters
and memory is drowned in now. Alas,
my childhood songs have been reduced to mutters.
Like wind that comes to mumble at the shutters,
or clocks that run but don't keep proper time,
my tongue, once fluent, limps along and stutters.
Forgotten brilliance overgrown with rust –
the smell of rain engulfs the smell of dust.

AUGURY

Today was minutes longer than yesterday,
the Earth turns slow, tipping back towards the Sun.
Stars fall at strange angles and get hung up in clouds,
filling the sky with unfamiliar constellations
as if God had shaken a jewelery case
and left the chains tangled, pendants hooked together
dangling askew across the sky.
Augur, read me this riddle:
what planet rules the fortunes of empires?
Does it rise or set, or move at all
or is it trapped, like a scarlet fish in a net
of static history? Horrible thought.
Shake the box again, God. Roll the stars like dice
and let us read the numbers plain.

LEAVES OF GLASS

Ever since the sun first rose,
shining green through leaves
dancing in the dawn wind,
light like shifting stained-glass –

I've been sitting with this glass
or half a glass, of *vin rosé*
that I can't finish and won't leave.
How did I come to wind

up here, alone, listening to wind?
Will another turning of the glass
find me walking among roses
or sleeping under falling leaves?

By my elbow, my book's leaves
turn one by one in the wind.
Too delicate, this house of glass
to withstand the storm on the rise –

But better a green leaf in the wind
than a dried rose under glass.

INTERMISSION

Rain falls quiet in the dying wind
from clouds unfolding like tattered curtains
on the stage of sky. A new act begins
as new players stumble on, uncertain
of plot or script. They swirl breezes
like gauzy capes, costumes of no color.
Tread lightly, winds, give us a little ease.
Brush some warmth on the sky's bright pallor
where snow or sandstorm, frost or fire
hovers beyond the horizon of vision.
Last week's weather is now retired
leaving us, audience at intermission
poised like angels on the heads of pins,
watching for change in the dying wind.

A SHELF FULL OF TOYS

Where are the tall ships that used to fill this harbor?
Where are the sailor-men who walked these wharves?
Gone, gone like a herd of horses galloping across the wide sea,
gone like a flock of birds scattering into the storm.

Where is the city that used to crown this hill?
Where are the folk who thronged the busy streets?
Gone, gone like a sand castle foundering in the surf,
gone like a cloud of leaves carried in the wind.

Where is the dreamer whose long dream this was?
Who now will read the treasure-maps and ancient volumes of adventure?
Other hands will open the book and bring home the ships,
other soil is home to the seeds of the magic forest.

HARDENING

In my young days, the sap flowed thick
as honey, hardening to scabs
of amber. Now I've lost the trick
of flowing seamless round the stabs
and stings of life. The wood's grown hard.
My rings are narrower each year,
confined by thickened bark and scarred
dead tissue, strictures too severe
for growth.

       My sweet child, you may gather
amber drops to string around
your neck – my memories of pain
become you. I'm content. I'd rather
let them go, let them be found
by others. My loss: someone else's gain.

BRASS AND CYMBALS

> "Though I speak with the tongues of men and of angels,
> and have not love, I am become as a sounding brass and
> tinkling cymbal."
>
> — I CORINTHIANS 13:1

Black jackal in the desert giving tongue
whose echoes shake the hanging cymbals
in the conqueror's tents: make faint their hearts!
Vengeful ghosts, come forth across the sand.

The hourglass empties itself of sand
as the minutes whisper from tongue to tongue.
We're no longer convinced by flags and symbols
for there's too much desolation in these hearts —

too much broken glass in these hearts
too much blood spilled on foreign sands
too many curse our names in foreign tongues.
You still mean us to march to drums and cymbals

but don't imagine that I speak in symbols
for these are the words of an angry heart.
You fed my generation on lies and sand.
Now we speak truth in the jackal's tongue.

Your tongue is sounding brass, a tinkling cymbal.
False prophet, your heart bleeds sand.

DRAGON'S EGG

A man went to the desert, seeking heat
to warm the cold stone egg he called a heart.
The sun blazed down, the sand blistered his feet.
He felt the stone grow warm, then split apart.
Then from his chest a sheet of flame unfurled
his flesh consumed, his bones to ashes burned.
And new-made, jeweled eyes looked on the world –
dead stone to living dragonet had turned.
Who knows what shape the soul will take, released?
For caged within these leaden lumps of clay
go angels, devils, strange and marvelous beasts
bizarre, miraculous and everyday.
Turn back and look – your footprints on the trail,
the marks of paws or claws or dragging tail.

A HOLLOW FLUTE

When all your busy striving comes to rest,
you'll find that you can make a clearer sound.
It's through a hollow flute that breath flows best.

No need for endless search or desperate quest,
the things you've lost will once again be found
when all your busy striving comes to rest.

Anxiety lets go your throat and chest,
a lifetime's worth of knots to be unwound.
It's through a hollow flute that breath flows best.

Like tired birds returning to the nest,
you'll fold your wings and settle to the ground
when all your busy striving comes to rest.

And after all, surrender's for the best.
In silence, there's a voice that can't be drowned.
It's through a hollow flute that breath flows best.

Perhaps these things can't really be expressed.
The heart's a frail reed, to bear this sound.
When all its busy striving comes to rest,
it's a hollow flute that breath flows through the best.

METAMORPHOSIS

Come, love: dive with me
into the well of silence. Eel-like,
entwined, we'll seek the dark.
Pioneers of lightless new metropoli
eyeless, finned and sinuous,
we'll know the ocean's currents within and without
with new senses, neither taste nor touch.

Already the transformation begins:
people go by in groups
stop and turn as one –
wet raincoats flashing in the light –
slip past and vanish.
Trees toss in slow-motion
while unseen surf thunders overhead.
At the corner a ragged man
with the mad blind stare of an ancient sturgeon
mutters: "Watch for sharks."

We were ever drifters. Call me jetsam.
Call me homeless, plankton, glass-shelled diatom,
larval oyster, alien, Sargasso eel, transient,
microscopic citizen of a different kingdom.
Monstrous adulthood approaches:
time to colonize, set down some byssae*
or learn to swim.

---

* Plural of *byssus*, a mass of strong silky threads that mollusks such as mussels
us to attach themselves to rocks and other hard surfaces (*Encarta College Dictionary*)

THANK GOD FOR SLEEP

Thank God for sleep, that separates the days
one from the next. You know it doesn't pay
to keep them chained together. We could stay
forever in a land of tense regret
forgiving, but unable to forget
or move ahead. It's time to press "reset"
and go to bed, and let the daytime go.
Tomorrow starts anew, and lets us show
we're not the prisoners of the things we know.
Exhaustion wraps around me like a quilt,
a haze that swallows anger, grief and guilt,
the things I broke today, the things I built –
now all surrendered, fading to a heap
of broken images. Thank God for sleep.

THAT'S LIFE

You live in a glass house. By all means throw stones.
Break it down from the inside –
any hatching chick does as much.
There's no room for wings inside that shell.

Now you'll get wet from the rain,
burned by the sun,
frozen in winter. That's life.
Life under glass is not worth living.

Break the bell-jar – who knows what's inside?
It takes fire to hatch a phoenix egg
or open a jack-pine cone and scatter the seeds.
Fire, death, destruction
bring forth life.

SILENCE, SWALLOWS, BRIDGE

The dark swirl of water under the bridge
when no answers echo in the unfurling wind
and the empty sky rings with utter silence –
blueness marked only by the darting of swallows,
unrelieved by clouds. The absence of writing
on the summer sky. The unbearable weight

of time filled with nothing but waiting,
of the story endless and unabridged,
of the search for meaning. Have we no right
to demand a signpost or two along the winding
of our paths? It's a bitter thing to swallow,
that all the answer we'll ever get is silence.

Too long, too long standing in silence
too long in the company of those who wait
and do nothing. Too much time swallowed
by watching travelers cross the bridge,
watching boats set their sails to the wind.
Too much that cannot now be set right.

Each time I take up my pen to write
my words disappear into endless silence
like feathers carried in a careless wind.
It's unbearable, to be so weightless.
Rust flakes and paint peels from the bridge
and mist rises from the river to swallow

the pylons where the nesting swallows
rest, perching, though the ancients wrote
that they have no feet. Under the bridge
the homeless encampment watches in silence.
There's nothing for them to do but wait
for warm weather, an end to the wind.

If only I were at home in the wind
footless and winged like a swallow,
there would be no need to stand and wait
there would be no need to sit and write.
If only I were at home in the silence
I could get up and cross this bridge.

The bridge seems frail to bear my weight
and my nervous swallow can't break the silence.
I'll write the end of this story on wind.

JOURNEYING

THE NEW QUEST OF THE DARK TOWER

Oh I have known this, your sky bleeding smoke, forever.
No guarantees were offered by yesterday's newspaper
whispering against the curb this morning when the sky
was lilac and windless, threaded with silent crows.
No guarantees were offered, childe-hero
in the wasteland of tomorrow's sale windows
in the sterile dance of the mannequins
posing frozen, announcing the change of seasons.
Plate-glass shivered at the sound of your horn
but this isn't Jericho. We need a different way in
to the city's hearts. We need doors with fun-house mirrors
that see around corners. We need a flight of crows for raucous augury.

You have known this forever. The shadow under the porch light.
The furtive movement behind the hedge. Laughter from passing cars.
The smell of death under the kitchen sink. This is your heritage:
the weight at the bottom of your backpack
the brown stain drying on the heel of your shoe
the crisscross tracks on the sidewalk. No animal guide.
You're on your own in the frozen maze of the walls of the city
lined with carnival mirrors.

I have known this forever: no-one's exempt from being a hero.
No city without a desert and a dark tower.
Questing yesterday, questing tomorrow and *always* questing today –
a movable feast, spread at your feet every lilac dawn.
Left to be gnawed by rats among the litter
of yesterday's news and tomorrow's sales.

The piper offers cut-rate extermination, but no guarantee
unless you pay in full. Make no bargains.
Learn to play the music of the crows on your horn.
Look in the shivering mirrors for someone else's face,
your face, stretched around a corner.
Your eyes, bleeding smoke. Your eyes full of lilacs.
Tomorrow's for sale, but you have to pay today.
There are no guarantees. There's no new news.
We've known this story forever.

COMET IN THE SKY

Orbiting in distant darkness
like a snowball thrown by God,
comet goes its route unchanging.
Till one day, attracted sunward
it lets go its hold on sky,

plummets towards the inner planets.
Boiling ice pours into vacuum.
Shrinking, burning, comet leaves a
twisted trail of glitter-dust
laid across the vault of sky.

See it pass with mad hair streaming,
seeking final dissolution,
blazing in the sun's embrace –
like a soul approaching God
through the empty halls of sky.

IN, THROUGH, OUT

It was only an open door,
why was I afraid? It was just a door,
with rusting hinges and paint peeling from the jamb.
It hung a little crooked,
and I couldn't see beyond –
but I could hear.

Music.

I think it was music.

I think I smelled roses
like wine
and jasmine
like birdsong
I think I heard music.

I remember wanting to dance.

If only the door had been closed
I would have banged on it
kicked it in frustration
demanded to be let in
to savor the roses
and maybe join the dance.

But it was open
and if I had looked
I would have gone in
through
out.

IN THE DARK

I close my eyes and see them burning in the dark
human souls like blazing bonfires in the dark.

The path runs straight, it's we who build a labyrinth
and puzzle over threads we've strung in the dark.

No lamp or candle guides the moth tonight, I fear
she's flying blind like me, and groping in the dark.

The sun has gone, the moon is new, but we have stars
enough for us to find our way home in the dark.

I write my prayers on slips of paper, smooth them flat
and let them burn to ghostly ashes in the dark.

WHITE SPACES

Look at all the white space on this map:
Unknown, uncharted, probably desolate lands
"Here Be Monsters" written in some ancient hand.
What brave explorer might fill in these gaps?
I say I can.

Well, how bad could it be? just empty spaces.
Not to brag... I've been some dangerous places.
I've waded quicksands and walked desert trails.
Where others disappeared without a trace,
I never failed.

Incognita, this terrain... yet it reminds me
of something I've forgotten, or perhaps never seen.
Each morning of this expedition finds me
staring ahead at some familiar scene
I'd thought behind me.

This landscape mingles dream and memory.
Impossible, here in deep desert, I can hear the sea
or a cool breeze smells of mountain air and pines.
If these are memories, they are not mine
not drawn from me.

I've found some tracks, but whose? I fear to guess.
They fit my shoes... by now, that's no surprise.
Whatever I once knew, I now know less
but know the truth, this waste's a thin disguise
a mask of lies.

Yes, I remember. Yes, I've been here before.
I was the wanderer shipwrecked on this shore.
I met You here, and then I went away.
We always knew that I'd come back once more
this time to stay.

WALK IN HIS TRACES

I dreamed I was walking in the desert,
there were footprints in the dust of the trail.
I stepped in them and found myself dancing.

One gate stood open in an iron fence,
on it, the mark of a hand.
When I touched it sparks flew.

In the noise and confusion of the crowd
I heard a voice whisper:
"La illaha il Allah."
I turned and saw no-one, only footprints
and the city shone with brilliant light.

The world bears witness to the presence of a few —
walk in their traces.

THE TRUTHSEEKERS

They tell of a blind girl lost in the desert.
Lions guided her from waterhole to waterhole.
When she slept, vultures spread their wings to shade her.
Snakes and scorpions kissed her feet with kindness.
Years passed.

The king of a nearby kingdom heard of this woman.
"I'll find out the secret paths of the desert from her.
Caravans will pass in perfect safety, my kingdom grow rich.
My armies will move in stealth against my enemies.
Bring her to me!"

He sent ten soldiers into the desert. None returned.
He sent a hundred soldiers into the desert. None returned.
He sent a thousand soldiers into the desert. One returned,
half-starved, half-blind, half-mad with thirst.
This is his tale:

"O King, I've seen the woman you sought.

Bandits fell on us by night.
We cut each other down in the confusion of the fight.
Our battle churned the earth to scarlet mud.
The greedy moon drank down our fresh-spilled blood.
Morning came with its merciless light.

One man in five lay dead, and none could know
whether the hand that slew him was friend or foe.
Over them we raised a burial mound
and our captain said: "We'll go
forward until this woman's found."

Then, a corner of the sky turned brown.
We found no shelter. Within the hour
a sandstorm fell on us with all its power.
Half our men and all our animals were devoured
by blowing sand, or swallowed by the ground.

Our captain was unmoved by the disaster.
"In the King's name, our Lord and Master,
we'll complete this task at any cost.
What though all our animals are lost –
without them, we'll travel even faster."

We moved like locusts across the sandy waste.
The last man found each waterhole drunk dry.
We strove to make haste
under a pitiless blazing sky.
The desert is a terrible empty place...

Most often, our scouts never came back.
We thought them taken by lions,
as every sand patch showed us lion tracks.
The captain shouted: "No alliance!
These creatures show only witless defiance!"

Men were stung by scorpions and died raving.
Men fell to the tawny sand snake's bite.
Men thirsted, and killed for the craving,
or cut their throats by night
rather than endure another daylight.

How many men were left... I could not say.
Thirst, horror, desolation, complete disarray
of mind and body, reason stripped away...
I mean, I'd forgotten counting
when we found the woman by a fountain.

O King, I've found out what you wished to know.

I've looked on the eyeless face of Truth.
We fell at her feet and groveled like slaves.
Too dry for tears, yet our hearts wept.
She held up a mirror –
no tongue can tell all the terrible things I saw.

O King, it is not the path that keeps you safe but what you bring to it."

A king throws away his crown and leaves his land,
walks alone into desert in a starless night.
What eyes watch from the shifting sands?

Upward the path, winding into light.
Windblown dust hides his tracks.
Gone beyond human sight.

Will he ever come back?

LEAD TO GOLD

Turning lead to gold was just
a bonus of alchemy's quest –
the prize was everlasting life.
It seems they chose eternal strife
instead of eventual rest.

No – those were just ideas, dressed
in symbols, not made manifest.
Which cuts, the sharpness or the knife
in turning lead to gold?

He turned away, still unimpressed.
His marching style seemed addressed
to different drum or other fife.
Abandoning scholastic life,
he took the path he found the best
that turning, led to gold.

JOURNEY

I. NO DIRECTIONS

No-one will draw you a map
of what's around the corner, under the hedge,
behind the door, behind your back, behind your eyes
closer to you than your jugular vein.
Travel by subtle ways.
Embark at the stations of the heart.
Your ticket's in hand. The board says:
GOD TRAIN LEAVING NOW
ALL PLATFORMS OPEN SEATING
All aboard.

II. THE FINE PRINT

Don't expect to find
yourself. More likely
you will lose your mind.
Don't hold on too tightly.
Leave the baggage in the baggage car.
Go lightly.
Don't remember where you are.
Let someone else remind
you that you've come so far —
and don't expect to find
yourself.

III. COMPANIONS

Come join us and we'll journey to the East.
We'll break the idols and expel the Beast,
and every member of our fellowship
at journey's end will join in joyous feast!

But soon enough we fell into dispute
when all of us were challenged to refute
some point Thursday – or was it Chanticleer? –
had made about the message – or the route –

No matter; I forget, or cannot mention
what caused that endless, miserable dissension
that broke our will and severed friend from friend
and made a mock of all our good intentions.

We set out to make the world a better place.
It seemed a good idea, on its mere face.
Where'd we get lost? Why are we wandering
in houseless, hopeless, pathless, empty space?

IV. THE SIX OF SWORDS

It's supposed to mean leaving conflicts behind,
finding a solution, getting a good plan,
clearing a troubled mind...
You get help from the ferryman,
though no-one seems to know what kind.

The gypsy didn't like the Six of Swords.
"*Bad luck. Conflict. Journey over water.*"
It's not a proper boat, just a pile of boards.
And the vicious ocean gives the quarter
that a lamb gets at slaughter.

Now I'm clinging to a single plank.
It serves to keep my head above the waves.
So far I've been spared a watery grave,
but fear that all my fellow travelers sank –
I saw none of them saved.

V. THE VERY OLD TORTOISE
Where do you think *you're* going?
How can you arrive someplace you never left?

Listen: Oppenheimer tried to take me home for his kids.
I said: "Put me right back.
You've meddled with the world enough for one man." He did.

Darwin learned all about change from his finches.
I taught him stillness
(and how to live on earthworms in a pinch).

And Achilles, red and shouting
(I almost said, *pouting*) at the finish line:
"How the *hell* did you get here ahead of me?"
Silly man, I was here all the time.

VI. THE GARDEN MAZE

This garden's overgrown and gone to seed.
The hedges are tall and heavy, hung with thorns.
The sundial casts no shadow.
Faceless statues point to the center of the maze:
there's a dry pool beneath a broken arch of stone.
Which way did I come? Which way to go?
Show me the straight path
I pray, *show me the straight path.*

Somewhere a robe whispered on the paving.
Nothing was there when I turned at the sound,
but the hedges murmured of mysterious passages
and water flowing underground
down
down
down, through the dust-choked throat of stone
where Alph meets Styx and words are all forgotten
the only memories are graved on whitened bone.

VII. SILENCE

The temple bell rings.
Between reverberations
you can hear silence.

YOU'VE BEEN WALKING

You've been walking, town to town,
madman, sinner, saint or clown.
Drunk on wine, or desert air?
Full of joy or sick despair?
Guest with me; come in, sit down.

Did you find your soul at the Lost and Found?
Did you dig your roots out of sacred ground?
Was there holiness in the places where
you've been walking?

You're coming back the long way 'round,
You've seen the light and you've heard the sound.
It left its mark in your silent stare,
a window open on a soul stripped bare.
Lost wayfarer, homeward bound –
you've been walking.

IN THE LAND OF ILLUSION

SESTINA, INSPIRED BY RUMI

> These words I'm saying so much begin to lose meaning:
> existence, emptiness, mountain, straw: words
> and what they try to say swept
> out the window, down the slant of the roof.
>
> —JELALUDDIN RUMI (VERSION BY COLEMAN BARKS)
> KULLIYAT-E SHAMS #950

Atop the mountain,
a hut of straw.
It has one window,
tight-thatched roof.
A barren existence
in windswept emptiness!

Searching for emptiness
I climb the mountain
tired of existence
that's barren as straw –
forsaking roofs,
seeking windows.

Come to the window,
look out on emptiness.
Here at the world's roof,
atop this mountain,
the wind blows straws
over the edge of existence.

And what is existence?
Just a window
into a world made of straw.
Beneath it, emptiness.
We think it solid, the mountain
but it's a flimsy roof.

We'll shelter under any roof,
clinging to existence
beneath some mountain...
Turning away from windows,
fearing emptiness,
clutching at straws.

Burn every straw.
Leave your roof.
Truth is emptiness,
the illusion is existence.
Fly from your window
to the top of the mountain.

Existence. Emptiness.
Mountain. Straw.
Window. Roof.

SHATTERED SNOWGLOBE

The sky is grey-white glass, a windowpane
that's frosted, etched with acid, stung by sand
to keep out peering eyes. But don't complain –
we live inside a snowglobe. Someone's hand
will shake it up. The sky will clear, and soon
the sun will shine, relentless glare of fire,
or else we'll see a peeking, gibbous moon
a wicked, half-closed eye.
                                        Remake entire
this sorry scheme of things! Captivity,
pinned on a card, pressed under glass, confined
by our perceptions of reality,
by frosted glass that stunts a half-grown mind!
The sleeping Dormouse wakes up as a Hatter.
We spread our wings and make the snowglobe shatter.

DEAR DIGORY

Dear Digory: you write with news of Narnia
as if you still expect me to believe it's true?
Years ago we made up and played a child's game
about rings, pools, a witch, a wood,
gold and silver trees that grew from coin-seeds,
your uncle mad, your mother dying.

We invented red-sunned Charn, a dying
world, as well as newborn Narnia.
Perhaps you'd gleaned some fantastic seed
of all this fairy-tale from your uncle's books, true
scholar he (though apt to lose the wood
for the trees). He played ugly games.

One part of this that was no game –
you really thought your mother was dying.
I'll forgive much for that – but if you would
only abandon this obsession with Narnia!
What life could be based on something so untrue?
False flower grows from false seed.

Yes, this and only this has been the seed
of our separation. This childhood game.
Because you insisted and insisted it was true,
long past time the dream should have been left to die.
I grew tired, Digory, of playing Narnia.
Your importuning fell at last on ears of wood.

You've followed your uncle's path (though I would
call you both wiser and kinder), seeking some seed
of knowledge that might lead you back to Narnia.
You've given up adult life for the game.
And as you've lived, you're determined to die,
still struggling to prove it was all true.

Is this how you hope to win my true
love, by leading me back to the wood
of make-believe, where hope can save the dying?
Too late; my heart's a dry shriveled seed.
Digory, release me from this game.
It was you I loved, and never Narnia.

Polly, the wardrobe was wood that grew from the seed.
Though dead, it's magic enough to prove the truth –
children playing games can still find Narnia.

ESCAPE FROM TIME AND SPACE

The sundials have stopped. The compasses are broken –
pendulums hang out-of-joint from frozen gears.
Bells hang still above the graveyards where the awoken
dead sit and chatter news of the terrible years.

From the middle of nowhere to the edge of nowhen, go.
My wounds are sown with salt; I burned
all the maps. There will be no return.
Time to hitch, 'cause walking's most too slow.

KLEIN SPACE

I cannot jump through all these inky hoops.
I made a Möbius strip, all nice and neat.
I'm trapped and struggling in these twisted loops.
A paper strip, half-twist, the loop complete.

I made a Möbius strip, all nice and neat.
I thought I'd walk it to some destination –
a paper strip, half-twist, the loop complete
a magic aid to higher navigation.

I thought I'd walk it to some destination,
but cursive scrawls were drawn across my trail.
A magic aid to higher navigation
that I was confident would never fail –

but cursive scrawls were drawn across my trail
like vines of ink, that twined around my feet
that I was confident would never fail.
My Möbius shortcut led me to defeat.

Like vines of ink that twined around my feet
I'm trapped and struggling in these twisted loops.
My Möbius shortcut led me to defeat.
I cannot jump through all these inky hoops.

THE ELEVATOR AT THE END OF TIME

In the tower at the end of Time there's an elevator
whose buttons are not marked with numbers. They say
Home, Mezzanine, Ground, and other things
but most of them don't work —
the elevator doesn't go, or stops
between floors, and you can't take the stairs. Every layer
is just another layer.
The top button says *Out*
or *Up and Out*
or *Beyond the Sky*, or *Behind the Veil*
— anyway, it's not helpful. But it's the only one lit.

Look again. The words on the buttons shimmer,
dissolve, swirl into alien glyphs
then disappear. The row of buttons gleams enamel-white
like knuckles on a skeletal hand, or polished teeth
except the top one, which reads
Truth.

NO BOAT, NO WAVES

You are a tiny boat, tossing on the waves
rising and falling.
There is no boat. You are the waves
rising and falling.
There are no waves. Just the rising
and the falling
still.

MISFORTUNE

Seven years bad luck
illusions of self shattered
by falling mirror.

LOVE IN THE LAND OF ILLUSION

Come, let us two meet, touch, and part
among the hanging veils of which these walls are made.
Come, let us speak on matters of the heart.
Separate, we're joined by space.
We are both mask and masker, at this masquerade.
There's but one Face.

TRAVELING SOULS

Two dreamers met upon a windswept shore.
I know you.
                    Yes.
                              We dreamed this once before.
Are we awake or dreaming?
                         Yes.
                                   Let's dance.
The wind erased their footprints from the sands.

Two swallows fluttered underneath a bough.
We're here.
                    Again.
                              Awake and dreaming now.
But soon we'll be asleep —
                              Again.
                                   Let's fly.
They left their passage marked upon the sky.

Two salmon passed each other in the deep.
You're dreaming.
                    Yes.
                              Remember, in your sleep.
We've waterfalls to climb.
                         Yes.
                                   Let's go.
They wrote their wisdom on the water's flow.

We're two.

        We'll wake.

                At rising of the sun.

We'll be only One.

SHE SEES WHITE HORSES

She looks quite ordinary,
brown hair in braids or a bun,
neat dress, sensible shoes.
Cheerful and competent, unremarkable.

In her dreams, she sees white horses.

White horses pass in the street below.
Their riders throw roses at the balcony,
but they fall unregarded in the street.
Jasmine twines the balcony rail.

In her dreams, she sees white horses.

Always overlooked when present,
her absence created some concern.
Someone else would have to do her job —
but whyever would she go away?

In her dreams, she sees white horses.

When they searched her desk at work,
they found no note, no photographs
no sign of human occupation.
Her apartment smelled... ever so faintly... of jasmine.

In her dreams, she sees white horses.

FALLING STARS

I. Exile
Echo, echo
faint footsteps on the floor.
I came this way before
but memory fails and fades to shadow.
Shadow falls behind me
too faded to remind me.
The gate was closed and strangler-figs grew over it
my footsteps hidden by the fig-leaf's fall.
In fall the leaves are echoes of themselves.
When mirrors fall they shatter and your face goes with them.
Fragments of me stare from mirrors crazed.
Wherever I'm from, it isn't here.
Lost on the sidewalk
at home with waste
drunk on the serpent's tears.
Roses dot the killing floor like splashes of fresh blood
lichen claims the concrete kingdom. Life's tough.
Even in the garden, the jungle's near
both rose and lichen know the fear
of falling.

II. Captivity
Time is a poor guide,
his hands point a different direction every hour
like swinging scythes beheading flowers.
But you're stuck with him for the ride.

Clocks gnash their teeth inside,
though their faces show vacuous smiles.
You get truer time from sundials
gnomon shadows pointing time and season
linear hands of reason
laid across the face of denial –
denial of fear, denial of rage.
Raving captive in Time's cage,
you scream and stamp and shake the bars
but there's no escaping age
even hurtling lightspeed through the stars.

III. Dreaming
We cannot help but dream of flying.
Time, space and gravity
(these things we call reality)
obscure all clarity and make us dream of flying.
Full of fear and doomed to dying
we dream of light and air and open skies above
of endless love and endless flying.
Full of grief and crying, we dream of flying through the stars.

IV. Phaethon's Ride
Father, the sky is huge.
I lost the path. Now the horses run wild
up and down, scorching the earth.
I see melting wax, a falling child.
I see so much from up here –
Titan shadows rise from the land

and bend to peer at me in your chariot
with thunderbolt in hand.
To drive the Sun-god's car
was not my calling.
My aspirations cannot lead to the stars,
this stanza too will end
in falling.

V. Inversion
In the deepest well
drop a bucket at midday
and draw up the stars.

EARTH AND SAND

It happened last night. This morning
I woke to find the bedroom full of sand,
marked with the delicate webbed tracks
of some creature native not to earth,
but air and water. Some bird, it could be
but not one I've ever (waking) seen.

I have no time for the unseen –
there's work to do every morning,
and if I let it go, I could be
overwhelmed, drowned in the quicksand
of everyday life on earth.
My job is waiting – better make tracks!

A line of cars at the railroad tracks
waiting to cross – a sight I've often seen.
As I wait my turn, my mind unearths
memories of the hour before morning.
We were walking side by side in the sand.
You said, "It could be..."

What was it? What did you say could be?
Who were you, to leave mysterious tracks
on my heart? I count minutes like sand
grains in an hourglass. I stare unseeing
waiting for evening to swallow morning
and dreams to cover the earth.

I've always been so down-to-earth.
Not really the type who could be
found in bed dreaming all morning –
or wandering off to explore the trackless
untrodden shore of an unseen
ocean, over dunes of invisible sand.

But my shoes are damp and crusted with sand
and I'm losing my hold on solid earth
drowning under the weight of the unseen.
My dreaming echoes with sounds that could be
surf on rocks, or night trains on the tracks
and salt stains my pillow in the morning.

Into the bright morning I follow your tracks
believing you could be real, though never seen –
one foot on earth, one foot on sand.

AT THE FOOT OF THE WORLD TREE

A seeker said: "The World Tree has blight.
Her roots are gnawed by grubs, the wood inside
by beetles. Even now, her branches crack
and soon she'll fall, and let in endless night."
"That's nonsense!" cried a second, "She is hale!
Her boughs are hung with suns that do not fail,
she's rooted deeper than the worlds we know
and watered from a well that's never stale!"
The third one said: "The Tree you two dispute —
though sick or healthy, leaf or branch or shoot —
is mere illusion, painted gauze. Behold!"
And ripped the canvas wide. They stood struck mute —
then one by one, the disputants passed through
and so they disappeared, all three, from view.

WITH THE BELOVED

CARTESIAN SKY

Let me be X and let us solve for *why* –
for Y, I mean, the quantity unknown.
For X is humble, horizontal, prone
beneath the looming vertical of Y.
I may not dare to touch Cartesian sky –
my X is limbs and body, flesh and bone –
but I am seeking mysteries new-grown,
imaginary homes for such as i.

If we solve Y, or *why*, it's not enough
for solid proof. More unknowns intervene,
like *who* and *how*, and *what* remains unseen.
This last equation take on faith, with love:
As God is infinite, let X be me.
Let X at last approach infinity.

BURNING BREATH

If I were ever to lay eyes on my Beloved,
surely every tear I shed thereafter
would reflect in miniature His perfection.
If I were to hear the voice of God,
surely every word I spoke thereafter
would ring with the sound of His greatness.
If I were to draw a breath of my Beloved,
surely every exhalation of mine thereafter
would savor of His sweetness.

And, as breath is burning
every breath would burn away a little more of "me"
until nothing is left but God's breath
circling, echoing,
singing praise.

IF I HAVE FORGOTTEN

Now, as I peer among strange reflections
push through the wide-eyed throng – what have I forgotten?
Now, as I wander uncharted pathways
fading among hidden hedgerows – what have I forgotten?
It was just here –
there, somewhere –
underfoot, outside in, on the tip of my tongue,
closer to me than my jugular vein.
Now, as I swirl the leaves in my cup
and watch the clouds and the flight of birds – what have I forgotten?
What have I lost?
Surely it was a Name,
the Name that was breathed in the trees
the Name that the surf roared
the Name that echoed in the cave
the Name that the rolling earth writes on the heavens.

If I have forgotten the Name of my Beloved,
let Him whisper it in my sleep.
If I have forgotten the Name of my Beloved,
let Him write it in the smoke.
If I have forgotten the Name of my Beloved,
let Him draw taut the strings of my heart –
and play it!

LEARNING TO REMEMBER

The unforgetting know nothing of memory,
time past is always present, always now,
not another country but the house next door –
you have to lose something in order to find it.
We are learning to remember.

Do you remember
when we were stars and the night sky
was full of darkness and endless possibility?
And the evening and the morning were the first day;
do you remember when we came down
to the new earth
and walked among rocks and hills
that had not forgotten how to speak
and we joined their song.
We walked under the first tree –
or did we dance? Well, there was no difference then,
walking was dance, speech was song,
breathing was praise, for we had not learned
how to forget. That came later,
as creation ate up potential
and time consumed eternity
and infinity was filled by space –
as we were asked to wrap ourselves in veils
of illusion called flesh; and to forget, that we might learn
how to remember.

The unforgetting know nothing of memory.
Fortunate are the forgetful, who understand
the work of remembering. Fortunate are the wanderers,
who know the joy of coming home.
We are learning to remember.

APPRECIATION

How can mere clay appreciate the potter
whose hands have shaped it, strong upon the wheel?
Do fish appreciate their world of water?
How can mere clay appreciate the potter –
how can a wondering soul know God? Oh, daughter,
who's seeking knowledge, ask this as you kneel:
How can mere clay appreciate the potter
whose hands have shaped it, strong upon the wheel?

DEAD-LETTER OFFICE

I am sorry to tell you that your prayer has been judged insincere
and has been sent off to the dead-letter office of prayers
where the angel whose job it is will sort and file it
and close the drawer on its thin helpless squeaking. But...
the good news is, should at some future time you reconsider
and reoffer this prayer with a contrite heart,
the drawer will burst open, the file cabinet explode,
the door of the dead-letter office blow off its hinges
and all your dead-letter prayers in one gigantic flock will
(like starlings swarming up from a freshly plowed field
or herring back when their schools darkened the waters
and were considered a navigation hazard)
fly up darkening the sky with their numbers
and with intention as single as a Zen arrow
land in God's lap
and deliver their petitions.

SPIDERWEB

I thought I'd weave a web to hold my loved ones close
keep them whole, keep them safe from harm.
So I spun out shining threads of prayer.
One to my husband – it didn't have to go far.
One, but double-thick, to my parents.
One each to friends and family,
co-workers, colleagues, people I've met...
a forest of threads spun out from me.

Then I walked the spiral and laid down more thread,
but it didn't seem to stick together.
So at each crossing-point, I left a tear.
So the circles went.
The first few rounds were fine,
but as I spiraled out, the circles grew
and the radials were further and further apart
and I was getting tired...

"Help, God! I'm out of thread,
I'm out of tears!"

God lifted me from the unfinished web.
"Little spider, there's no need for this,
I have them all in the palm of My hand."

DEPTH

I'm floating on the ebb-tide. I'm resting in brine.
I'm resting at the bottom of the beach.
Can we go lower, God
deeper into the sea? I'm trying to learn the way
down. Weighed down. Way down.
No longer buoyant.
Diving, let go the air in strings of silver bubbles
let go, let be. There's so much depth
around the rapture.
Deep trenches lined with deeper secrets, pressure
weight of water pressing down
down on my head –
sole, flatfish, flounder, floundering flattened soul.
Lord, is this what it takes to learn
humility?

TRUTH

The truth will set you free, they say.
What they don't tell you is this:
The truth will not ask your opinion.
The truth will drag you by your hair, kicking and screaming.
The truth is a harder master than any lie.
The truth is a path with no end.
The truth won't hold your hand or dry your tears.
The truth tastes bitter as often as sweet
is dark as often as light
is heavy as lead and hard to grasp as a feather.

I spin helpless in the dirt, wheel of flesh
turning on the axle of Truth –
blinded by dust of my own making.
Truth, my Master, you drive me hard.

THIRST

You forget water
fall in love with reflections
and complain of thirst!

CHALKBOARD

Your mind's a chalkboard
scribbled full of stuff. Wipe it!
Let God write something.

INSIDE OUT

Is your heart too small
to hold Allah? No problem –
turn it inside out!

RAMADAN

Red sky burns to ash
around the New Moon's cradle.
Ramadan begins.

FASTING

The edge of the day is studded with wine-colored shards.
The edge of the day is strung with silver ornaments.
Hunger stalked us all afternoon
and now our heads ring hollow and dizzy like high towers.
The bells in our heads ring: *Praise God. Praise God.*
Praise God for cold bright air
      cold bright water
      darkness, food, light of lamps
      at the edge of the day.

YOU JUST MISSED HIM

I dreamed I sought my Beloved all through one sleepless night.
I thought I saw Him dancing amid fire and thorn.
The dark earth showed me the traces of His feet.
At the reflecting pool, only the moon looked over my shoulder.
The roses on the fence whispered of His passing:
"He was here." "No, here." "You just missed Him."

All night the garden murmured with His presence.
Hither and thither I pursued the rustling of His robe.
At dawn, alone and weary, I closed my eyes to rest.
At once He was there.

THE UNINVITED GUEST

He came unannounced to the party,
invited by – no-one knows.
He brought a bottle of wine, so we all shared,
got drunk
danced and sang.
What a scandal!
When morning came...
one forswore wine forever
one became a confirmed drunkard
one hanged himself from shame
one never drinks, but sings and dances all the time
one swore to go out and find our mystery guest
(whether to thank or harm, we weren't sure).
Most of us tried to put the whole thing out of our minds.
But I still wake sometimes at night
with the taste of wine in my mouth
and hear the echo of His laughter.

THERE YOU ARE

This vision came on me today, unlooked-for.

I stood at the heart of the urban wasteland, in an empty lot.
A car rusted on the corner, burned-out, its tires melted rags.
Trash was piled among the starving grass and shattered concrete curbs.
Broken glass and plastic. Worse things I won't mention.
The voices of the place all moaned of neglect and desolation.
I muttered: "Surely God is not here."

From nowhere a seed fell at my feet.
In the blink of an eye it split open and grew –
knotted roots upthrust the pavement at my feet –
the massive trunk overshadowed me –
and its limbs –

its limbs burned with the light of a million suns
its limbs were hung with countless worlds
its limbs were entwined with rivers of stars
its limbs filled endless space from edge to edge!

Its limbs murmured with the wind:
"I am here.
Even here, I am.

More:

Behold the tiniest twig on the tiniest limb
the tiniest green cell in the tiniest leaf.

There *you* are."

SURROUNDED BY DOORS

Sorrow is a gateway to Allah – so is joy.
Silence is a door to Allah – so is music
and both solitude and love are paths to Allah.
I am surrounded by doors, I can open none of them
for none of them are closed –
nor can I go out to meet my Beloved
for He is here.

GOD'S DANCE

God lives in every dance; the swirl
of water draining from the bath,
the logarithmic-spiral math
of nautilus in cells of pearl,
the curling traces left behind
by random particle decay,
the fractal fiddlehead display
of ferns beginning to unwind.

God lives in every dance; the crash
of guns on distant killing floors,
the refugees on foreign shores
who huddle over fires of trash,
the hopeless tears, the angry laughs,
the sirens racing through the dark,
the bloody thumb that leaves its mark
on missing children's photographs.

We search for truth in circumstance
and fear the world proves meaningless –
that life is ruled by random chance.
The good don't always find success
or wealth and health and happiness.
But still, God lives in every dance.

DOWN BY THE TEMPLE

It's quiet down by the temple
and yet the air vibrates as with thunder.
The bronze face of the gong ripples like water
kissed by breezes at sundown. *Hush!*
Do you hear the footstep,
see the sunflowers turn their heads
toward a brighter sun?
Do the silk banners stream out
reaching their painted hands
toward the approaching Guest?
Does the stone under your knees
reverberate: *Allah, Allah*
and your bones feel the echo
Allah, Allah
in the trembling bronze
Allah, Allah
and the whisper of silk
Allah, Allah
and the tears of flowers
Allah, Allah
and the stillness of air
Allah, Allah, Allah.

UNFORGETTING STONE

The forest falls behind. The icebound lake
is fringed with scree, and glacier-fathered streams
fall from the heights. In unremembered dreams
I've seen this place, but never while awake.
The clouds clear off, and clarity will break
my heart. Illusions ravel at their seams
illuminated by the light that gleams
on mountains. Plain the path that I must take

remembering a thing I've never known.
Forget myself. Go naked and unshod.
Forget the flesh, go just as breath and bone
for on the snow where never foot has trod
and on the bare and unforgetting stone
is written this: *There is no god but God.*

SHOUTING GOD

The hills above The Dalles
are striped with snow and last year's stubble.
Hawks hunt along the rows.
The hills were shouting God,
the trees were shouting God,
the fence-posts and frozen puddles
all joined the silent chorus.
The road under my wheels was shouting God,
and I too, I was shouting God,
God, God, there is no other.
The hills are shouting God!

Note: The City of The Dalles, Oregon, is situated in the north-central
part of the state on the Columbia River.

RETURNING

BITTER WELLS

A traveler walked along a desert track
surrounded by bare earth and bitter wells.
Her water gone, there was no turning back.
Mirages shimmered, deadly shining spells.

Past rocky hills where Manticora dwells
she toiled upward, downward, bent with care
over dead plains of dust and barren fells.
And when she looked ahead — no path was there.

Then sank she to the ground in dark despair
and wept for wasted progress, bitter shame:
"And have I come so far for this? *Unfair!*"
When least expected, then, an answer came.

"Oh child of mine, why all this bitter yearning?
Where all paths end, the heart begins returning."

ABOUT THE AUTHOR

Tiel Aisha Ansari is a Sufi, martial artist, and computer programmer. She was born in Philadelphia and lived much of her childhood in Tanzania. She has been writing poetry since her conversion to Islam in 2005. She lives physically in Portland, Oregon, where she works for a public school district; and electronically at knockingfrominside.blogspot.com.

Poetry of Daniel Abdal-Hayy Moore

Mars & Beyond

Laughing Buddha Weeping Sufi

Salt Prayers

Ramadan Sonnets

Psalms for the Brokenhearted

I Imagine a Lion

Coattails of the Saint

Abdallah Jones and the Disappearing-Dust Caper
(*Crescent Series*)

Love is a Letter Burning in a High Wind

The Flame of Transformation Turns to Light

Underwater Galaxies

The Music Space

Cooked Oranges

Through Rose Colored Glasses

Poetry of Tiel Aisha Ansari

Knocking from Inside

www.ingramcontent.com/pod-product-compliance
Lightning Source LLC
Chambersburg PA
CBHW020910090426
42736CB00008B/569